羅莎·帕克斯

Heroes and Role Models | Non-Fiction Series

Copyright © 2022 by Level Learning, INC. and Washington Yu Ying PCS™
Original and Edited Text Copyright © 2022 by Washington Yu Ying PCS™

All rights reserved. No part of this book in whole or part may be reproduced without written permission from the publisher.

Published by Level Learning, INC.

Content Contributors:
Washington Yu Ying PCS™
Level Learning - Jingyao Qi

Illustrations by: Matt Austin

Leveling classification based on Level Learning standard.
For full description, visit www.levellearning.com

ISBN 978-1-64040-042-9
Traditional Chinese Edition

About Level Learning:
Level Learning provides a literacy focused curriculum specifically designed for K-12 Chinese as a Second Language classrooms. Our program offers 20 levels of specific and detailed objectives, leveled texts and passages, mastery-based online assessment, and analytics to enable data-driven instruction. Level Learning reading curriculum for both literature and informational text emphasize grammar and comprehension skills to help teachers develop confident and independent Chinese language readers. The non-fiction series of books are specifically designed to support our informational text course based on multiple national standards. To learn more about our entire offering, visit www.levellearning.com.

About Washington Yu Ying PCS™:
Washington Yu Ying PCS is a Mandarin English dual language immersion International Baccalaureate (IB) World school. Yu Ying's mission is to inspire and prepare young people to create a better world by challenging them to reach their full potential in a nurturing Chinese/English educational environment. Yu Ying's comprehensive IB, dual immersion curriculum equips students with global competencies for success in the real world. As a leader in immersion education, Yu Ying is determined to advance Chinese language programs and global citizenry education by helping other schools create and strengthen their Chinese programs. For more information, email: products@washingtonyuying.org

羅莎·帕克斯是一位非洲裔美國人。她出生於1913年2月4日。

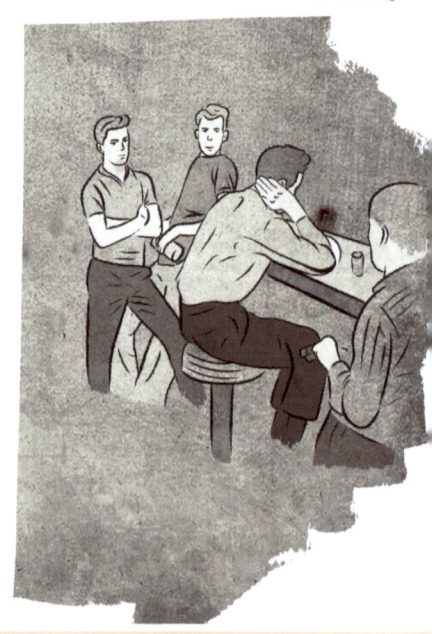

那時的美國很不平等。白人上白人的學校,非洲裔上非洲裔的學校。非洲裔不可以去白人的餐廳吃飯。

白人可以坐在巴士的前面，可是非洲裔要坐在巴士的後面。

羅莎·帕克斯覺得這樣不對。她覺得白人和非洲裔應該是平等的。

她在巴士上坐在白人的座位上。因為這件事，她被關了起來。

她很**勇敢**地說出這些不平等。因為她的努力，白人和非洲裔在巴士上可以坐在一起了。

羅莎·帕克斯改變了美國的歷史。她促進了美國白人與非洲裔的平等，讓美國變得更公平。

Glossary

	Pinyin	English Definition
非洲裔	fēi zhōu yì	African descent
平等	píng děng	equality
餐廳	cān tīng	restaurant
巴士	bā shì	bus
覺得	jué de	to feel
關	guān	lock up
勇敢	yǒng gǎn	brave
改變	gǎi biàn	to change
歷史	lì shǐ	history
促進	cù jìn	to promote

www.ingramcontent.com/pod-product-compliance
Lightning Source LLC
Chambersburg PA
CBHW041226070526
44584CB00001B/113